I0210978

FALLEN LOVE

poems by

Deirdre Garr Johns

Finishing Line Press
Georgetown, Kentucky

FALLEN LOVE

Copyright © 2025 by Deirdre Garr Johns
ISBN 979-8-88838-852-5 First Edition
All rights reserved under International and Pan-American Copyright Conventions.
No part of this book may be reproduced in any manner whatsoever without written permission from the publisher, except in the case of brief quotations embodied in critical articles and reviews.

ACKNOWLEDGMENTS

The following poems in Fallen Love have been previously published:

"Our Losses Are Softened" (original version published in *When Flowers Sing: A Poetry Anthology* by a thousand flowers, Spring 2024)
"Landline" (original version published by *Stone Poetry Quarterly*, November 2023)
"The Beginning of Something" (original version published as "Because Cell Phones Did Not Exist" by *Silver Birch Press*, February 2023)
"A Park in Gloucester City" (original version published by *Eunoia Review*, February 2022)

Publisher: Leah Huete de Maines
Editor: Christen Kincaid
Cover Art: Jennifer Hodges
Author Photo: Patty Schoelkopf-Lewis
Cover Design: Elizabeth Maines McCleavy

Order online: www.finishinglinepress.com
also available on amazon.com

Author inquiries and mail orders:
Finishing Line Press
PO Box 1626
Georgetown, Kentucky 40324
USA

Contents

To those we have loved

NOTE TO A SCHOOLGIRL CIRCA 1997

He passes me the note
palm to palm.

Such a note is not taken lightly—
words weigh heavy,
they almost can't contain
themselves.

Bathroom stall, graffiti walls.

I unfold the series of halves.

A few lines of print—
Can I give you a ride home?

When we find each other
in the crowded halls,
I return my reply
with a glance—
an ember in the eye—

and we walk palm to palm
to the gray-blue Lincoln
we would later call
periwinkle.

LANDLINE

7:30.

I scramble
to gather
shattered silence—
each ring a dart

no caller ID needed
before the *hello*—
breath held steady,
an inhale
before the dive

I sit back-to-back against the cellar door
my voice like a palm cupped around a hesitant flame,

I would float away if not for this cord, stretched beyond its reach—
unwound around corners, doors, halls—

coils straightened into an unnatural line,
certain to keep me
grounded

—for a boy calling demands
a certain kind of attention—

a connection made stronger
when the chance is taken
to make a call

to a girl waiting.

THE BEGINNING OF SOMETHING

We were strangers at sixteen
when you brought a single rose
to my house.

Directions given to drive through town,
down South Broad Extension into Schoeneck,
then Cherry Hill, first house on the right—

Gravel turning,
car door closing,
engine idling.

A knock on the back porch door.

I walk across the kitchen floor,
a staccato of steps,

and unlatch the metal slide—

cool air unable to calm
the flush of face,
like a smolder of sun at dawn,

and the rose—petals pulsed open:

a boy and a girl,
the beginning of something.

MARK OF AFFECTION

Our first date,
that day at the lake—
you invited me for a picnic
and a swim.

The silt on my feet—certain
to sink me.
I never did like soft spots.

I wrapped my legs around you,
an uncertain buoy.

You quoted somebody:
You can discover more about a person in an hour of play.

And committed the offense—
temptation and teeth meet.

I have watched this bruise
undress itself—
purple pushes past the surface,
red, feathered lines fade
into a jaundiced and remarkable shade
that has grown on me.

I applaud its ability to change
and remain.

A PARK IN GLOUCESTER CITY

I know no way around his hometown—
stuck between two cities,
constricted by the rise
of bigger things around it.

Row homes remain silent.

His third-floor apartment is stuffy,
and we have no patience
to wait for the window-unit.

I know a place
where we can find
some air.

We cross the street,
his fingertips against my wrist.

No headlights in sight.

Heat refuses to loosen
its grip.

Street lamps hum a lonely song.

Factory lights shutter the night sky.

We single-file down sidewalks,
buckled like toppled building blocks,
and turn off the main drag.

Our guide, an occasional porch light,
as night becomes closer to itself.

I could not find my way back
if I had all the light in the world.

We arrive at a playground
where I sit on a swing worn,
the rubber seat pinching the skin
of my inner thighs
in its cupped hand.

He pushes—
pattern deliberate,
release gentle,
nearly at rest
on return.

Momentum enough to move air,
our own orbit, small and bright.

SLEEPING WITH

We meet in the middle—
my hand rests upon your chest,
the perfect distance for whispers.

I note the rise and fall of your breath,
a lullaby—light and recognizable,
heavy with content.

I think about summer's first fireflies.
I'd run into dusk to chase them,
glass jar in hand,
a few sticks and blades.

I'd try to discover the secret of their light show.
Jar beside my bed, their soft glow
my companion.

Just as you begin to drift,
Are you asleep?

Eyelids flutter—
perhaps this will be
an all-nighter.

NIGHT TALKERS

This kind of heat is like a thick fog
you want to peel off in layers.

Small movements break a sweat.
We lie still
and apart.

We disagree on whether or not the open windows
let in a breeze, but leave them as is

because summer is still alive,
and I like to hear cars shuffle through the streets—
indistinct sounds that announce themselves at the corner stop—
and the scuffle of those who seek more than sleep,
their voices rise like chimes.

The intention to rest settles beneath the covers.

What else is there to do when night opens its arms?

Our words consume time,
and we attempt to cut and polish them
like rough gems—
but we come up empty-handed.

When night no longer drapes over us,
the sky lightens to a dull, bruised blue.

Sun and shadow mingle along slanted blinds,
the air changed and the ache of waking
somehow lighter.

MUSCLE MEMORY

The lamp on the desk is lit
low and our shadows soften
the cinder block wall.

I close my eyes
to smooth these knots—
follow the curve
to the top of your shoulder,
the strain of practice
on your back.

These muscles have a tendency to give.

I knead until my fingers
fall into skin soft
as warm paraffin.

I trace imaginary letters on your back
—H-I or B-Y-E.

Is sensation alone
enough
to follow?

You turn to face me.
Now, my palms on your chest.

What do I write in this field of down?

I begin to trace the letter X
over your heart,
but sink instead.

RAILS TO TRAILS

This ten-mile stretch weaves between sycamores
whose brown and green mottled leaves
remind me that life and death can exist
in one breath.

A dry stream that used to carry coal
from one town to the next is an empty vein.

Wooden posts guard this dry ditch,
waiting for water to soothe its core.

I wonder if the parched soil feels its loss.

We never make it more than three miles.

We rest against the posts.
You hug me
like a tightly knotted bow—
maybe you are afraid I will fall open
if you let go.
I smell the salt on your skin.

I squint through the naked trees
willing to give me a glimpse
into their emptiness,
and try to remember when some life
lingered between us.

UNLIKE THE STONE

I remember how the waters calmed
around the bend of boulders
and made wading to the middle simple.
We stretched our wet feet to test the depth.

There we chose stones to skip.
I admired them—
their necessity to yield,
their imperfections smoothed over and perfectly worn,
their willingness to be eroded by stronger forces.

I gave them up
to watch them walk on water,
to glide over something
that could never bear such weight.

How unlike the stone we are.

We become something to discard—
a thread or button tumbled under coins and paper clips,
into a drawer of whatnot
and lost among the others.

I think of those clear waters—

dull stones remain buried
below the surface shimmer,
unable to be retrieved,
and I wish I could bury that child's view
under dead flowers,
little tombstone for what is lost.

THE WALLS NEVER COME CLEAN

Yellow room—not of daffodils—

heavy with yellow air
and books with bindings bent

(pages cataloged for use
at a later date)

piled along the wall—
like a miniature leaning Tower of Pisa.

Your makeshift fortress—
standing room only—

the cigarette smoke enclosed
in papers sad and edges wilted.

I cannot help but feel the drag.

Then the disturbance.
You must get out of this *godforsaken town.*

Yellow room—empty.
No room for anything else.

But that aroma, that aroma.

WHEN THERE IS NOWHERE ELSE TO GO

These boxes do not stack even.
They lean delicate against each other
and wait to crumble—

clothes, books, shoes, makeup
do not puzzle-piece fit
into neat packages.

I gather them from the stoop
and place them in the back of a trunk too small.

I edge the key under the WELCOME mat
and drive north,
the turnpike opening itself
to deliver me home.

Old room—faded lavender,
knick-knacks and pictures
long since packed.

I draw the shades.
Light etched against the window frame remains
the last broken barrier.

I ball into the center of my childhood bed,
cover my head,
and wait for blackness,
a going under for surgery of sorts.

One forgets that life no
longer exists
but it is foolish to think
that home can return us
to a place
of unknowing.

SLEEPING WITHOUT

We used to meet in the middle—
a cushion to a fall,
a place to find warmth

and now, a void—
a phantom that lingers,
an emptiness that cradles everything,
an attempt to consume what dares move
into the middle.

I turn my back—
but the expanse laughs
at my attempt to suppress it
into something small
and unnoticeable.

I acknowledge the darkness,
a reverse psychology of sorts,
but it needs nothing
to fulfill it.

I am not ready to belong to myself.

I attempt to make amends with the edge of the bed,
but it offers no comfort—
reserved as an enemy line
when there was no middle ground to be found
before the emptiness.

My thinking wanders
too far to follow,
an overgrown path.

Who knew emptiness
could take up
so much space?

LONG DISTANCE CALLS

It is nearly midnight
when the phone rings.

I consider letting it go to voicemail,
a small gift that lets both of us
off the hook.

But I accept because you chose to call
and I did not.

You say you were studying,
something about *functions of the nervous system*—
something I can neither prove nor disprove,
a language that means nothing to me—

small talk meant to cushion
this crumbling charade.

I offer nothing and stare at a blank page
titled "distance makes the heart grow fonder."

It waits for words that never come.

My cursor blinks in sync
with this silent countdown.

It seems to wag its finger
as I wait for the hang up.

There is nothing to say.

The air is embarrassed by the quiet—
phone in hand,
line alive, then dead.

MARGINAL

Once upon a time,
you & I lived inside the margins—
I admired those heavy, black lines and occasional loop,
life attempting to burst open
for someone to notice.

Your command over the page, certain.

It all started with notes
torn from your Moleskine—
I'll be asleep but ring the bell when you arrive.
And later, *bronze key, red ring under the flower pot on the front porch.*

I became more permanent,
and so did the notes, appearing in the margins of books you wanted
me to read—
Tolstoy, Nabokov, Marquis de Sade.

I paged through while I waited for you
to get home from a night shift.

No margin of error in meaning—
you *make me mindless/*
forgetful except/
for you, Guinevere/
syllables can't lose/
themselves,
nor I you.

Now, you are a thousand miles gone.

You send me *The Complete Romances of Chrétien de Troyes*
and pen an inscription:
"Knights in shining armor no longer exist."

Words burdened by their own
dead weight—

we never made it/
til death do us part

Who can read between these lines—
perhaps a parting gift?

A rift that no pen strokes can repair—

how simple it is to disappear
and remain everywhere.

REMAINING FRIENDS

We sit empty handed and across from one another—
the booth a buffer that seems ready
to swallow me whole.

The clink of silverware against china distracts us.

I'll give you a call in a few days.

The late-night crowd makes it easy to sit silent,
voices loose like coins jangling helpless
in the bottom of a pocket.

The waitress asks if she can warm our cups.

Let's grab lunch soon.

Steam rises between us as we lean
closer to its warmth.

Condensation gathers on the rim
and slips away.

Better as friends.

This line frees us from a cement servitude—
we emerge as statues hollow,
tread heavy along a fine line,
and wait to be filled with dust
that will never settle.

Bandaged is easier to manage
than broken.

We'll just leave the door open.

The last bit of coffee, cold—
we wait for two separate checks.

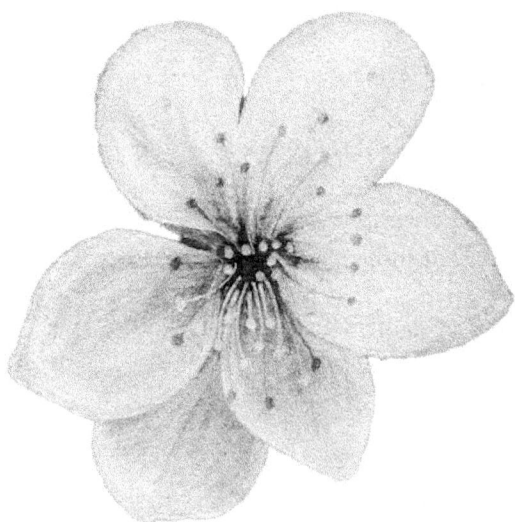

STILL

Photos taken with disposables
or pinhole cameras crafted from cardboard—
a casual collection to chronicle young love
now lies at box-bottom
under an off-white T-shirt
whose leftover scent of Polo
still frees itself upon rummaging.

Pink dress with heels in hand,
tux jacket loose over the shoulder.

Once in a while,
one is recovered
between the pages
of an old book—
misplaced acquaintances that keep each other company.

Like a forgotten game of hide and seek,
I'd like to think I placed this one with purpose—
a bench in the park,
cherry blossom petals like confetti,
picked and positioned solitary
behind my ear.

I am told to shred
these memories,
dead as they are.

How can I destroy what still has life?

A resting place will suffice—
exposed to light,
memories surface,
ripples in a still lake.

ADVICE GIVEN, NOT TAKEN

I walk to this silent altar
where boxes hold their contents
without judgment.

Tarnish grows old on sterling silver rings
that have outworn themselves.

Notes ironed open by hand,
words like *love, forever,* and *together*
hold no meaning.

People greet me with nods,
their experience a soft memory, and unknowing.

Sweep it under the rug.
Let bygones be bygones.

They offer this advice like communion,
expecting me to arrive with hands held open,
take it, and swallow.

And forget.

They do not see my heavy hands,
my offerings of loyalty
that cannot be discarded like dust
or dissolved in liquid.

A PLACE OF THE HEART

It's been a while.

I make the drive out I-80
during summer break.

Just a visit.

The odometer keeps thousands of these miles.

But I need no map for miles collected
like pressed rose petals—

I know where the last of the pines
speckle the mountainside
and recede into gentle hills
just beyond Danville.

Farms replace factories.
Radio stations can't decide
whether to stay
or go.

I take the exit for Route 322.

Silence is a familiar friend
on these roads that roam lonely.

I dial down the volume and wait.
Changing the station means
signal and reception
may never reunite—a chance I cannot take.

The sound is still down
when I pull into the gravel drive.

No curtains part
as I put the car into park.

Perhaps I am the only one
waiting for the return
of something.

A chance I have to take.

HABIT

The basement of the bilevel is familiar and nonchalant.
I set my bags on cushions thin and wicker brittle.

Dust covers scratches and stains on old tables—
leftovers, musty and alone.

These visits can no longer be counted
on one or two hands.

Everything is the same as I remember.

My first visit—wintertime in western Pennsylvania.
Icy roads and a long drive back to campus
meant stopping by your parents' house for the night.

That was the beginning.
Our time together and apart is one long memory,
woven and worn at the edges
like an old quilt—perhaps better left folded.

It is July now, and the air is heavy.

We keep company with comfort,
the heart unwilling to reason
with itself.

I admire the linoleum's tenacity
amid bruises.

I take my bags to the guest room.

Is there any room left
in a space where so much
has gone already?

OUR LOSSES ARE SOFTENED

The rose—once bloomed and watered—
is now faded and crumbled.

Dried petals pressed
between two heavy things,
thorns worn hollow and dull.

Petals disintegrate into dust—
edges smudged into something soft
and delicate of the past.

But time does not heal—
it only distances us
from memories
we struggle to forget.

And I wonder—did we not
crush ourselves into this fragility?

WHAT WE CANNOT HAVE

If I could call you by another name—
river returned full after drought,
white bird with bowed neck to drink from me,
sieve that catches the excess,
obsidian under water…
but we do not flow fluid.

We remain fixed in some predetermined dance—
one that will not permit us to partner.

I used to think I could control this momentum,
that galaxies intertwined along the edges
by some fused junction point that held them together
without concern for the space around or in between
and that I could spin myself directly into you

but we separate and circle each other,
repelled by something
invisible.

Unable to converge
or diverge,
we are meant to punish ourselves
for what we cannot have.

TO LET GO

The dandelion thrives
on its ability to die,
scattered chaos that lands where it can—
a haphazard path without worry.

It takes more effort
to cling to a core dried
than to let go.

I envy this kind of renewal.

Fluff—the stuff of childhood—
so delicate, taken by the wind
or a soft sigh,

releasing itself
like the slip of a shawl
over a bare shoulder.

With Thanks

I would like to thank those who took the time to read my poems-in-progress and offer their thoughts, especially Michelle Andis, Jessica Murante, Randy Sinsel, Marcus Amaker, Miho Kinnas, and Alex Yucas—your attention to the details is much appreciated. Thank you to Jonathan Stiffy and James Berry for your expertise on gems and music. Thank you to Frank Holland for the impromptu conversation about whatnot. Thank you to Jennifer Hodges for the beautiful illustrations. And, last but not least, thank you to Phil Terman for your words of wisdom, conversation, and encouragement.

Much of Deirdre Garr Johns' work is inspired by memories of people and places. Her writing often incorporates elements of the natural world to capture the common existence that we share and highlight the beauty of nature. Deirdre enjoys all types of writing, but poetry is a first love. To her, poems are like photographs that capture the essence of a time and a place and create a moment of inspiration and reflection in one's life.

Deirdre's poetry has appeared in *Sylvia Magazine, South Carolina Bards Poetry Anthology, Eunoia Magazine, Nymeria Magazine, Silver Birch Press, Stone Poetry Quarterly*, and more. Her nonfiction has appeared in *Sasee Magazine,* the Surfside Chapter of the South Carolina Writers Association personal essay contest, *Twists and Turns Personal Story Publishing Project*, and more. She has also published a children's book titled *Weathering the Storm* (2024).

Deirdre has lived in many places, but Pennsylvania will always be home. She currently lives in South Carolina with her family. Her website is *www.amuseofonesown.com*.

www.ingramcontent.com/pod-product-compliance
Lightning Source LLC
Chambersburg PA
CBHW022052080426
42734CB00009B/1306